Hockey

Hockey Made Easy

Beginner and Expert Strategies For Becoming A Better Hockey Player

By Ace McCloud

Disclaimer

The information provided in this book is designed to provide helpful information on the subjects discussed. This book is not meant to be used, nor should it be used, to diagnose or treat any medical condition. For diagnosis or treatment of any medical problem, consult your own physician. The publisher and author are not responsible for any specific health or allergy needs that may require medical supervision and are not liable for any damages or negative consequences from any treatment, action, application or preparation, to any person reading or following the information in this book. Any references included are provided for informational purposes only. Readers should be aware that any websites or links listed in this book may change.

Table of Contents

DEDICATED TO THOSE WHO ARE PLAYING
THE GAME OF LIFE TO
WIN
KEEP ON PUSHING AND NEVER GIVE UP!
Ace McCloud

Be sure to check out my website for all my Books and Audio books.

www.AcesEbooks.com

Introduction

I want to thank you and congratulate you for buying the book, "Hockey: Hockey Made Easy: Beginner and Expert Strategies For Becoming A Better Hockey Player."

Hockey is a fun and competitive sport that many people enjoy playing. During a game of hockey, two teams play against each other with the objective being that each team tries to score the most points by hitting the puck into their opponent's goal. There are several variants of hockey, including roller hockey, which is generally played on a paved street or wooden arena, field hockey, which is played on a field and ice hockey, the most popular variant, which is played on a skating rink. Hockey has been around as early as the era of ancient Egypt and truly began to take form during the nineteenth century.

Aside from being a fun sport that people of all ages can enjoy, hockey often provides many health and personal development benefits to its players. Hockey is a great form of physical activity that works out your entire body at once. It is great for improving your coordination, agility and flexibility as well as your physical strength and reflexes. Playing on a hockey team also helps to develop teamwork skills, including the ability to communicate, listen and respect others. Working on a team can help players to develop their self-confidence and patience, which is very important in sportsmanship and in other key areas of life.

This book contains proven steps and strategies on how to become a better hockey player by developing key areas of their life, including their health habits, body strength and mental abilities. In this book, first, you will discover how to select the best gear and equipment for optimal performance as well as how to properly stretch and warm-up before a practice, game or workout. You will then learn all of the best hockey-specific techniques that you can practice to improve your skills, both on and off the ice, so that you can work towards becoming a top player. You will also discover the secrets to a great hockey player's dietary and nutritional habits and how pairing those habits with strength training can help you excel at hockey. Finally, you will learn some of the best hockey-specific workouts and mental techniques that can help you become a well-rounded and dominant player .

Chapter 1: Gearing Up For Hockey

Helmet – Helmets are the best source of head protection in hockey. They protect your head from pucks traveling through the air, skate blades, stick checks and any other hazards that are posed on the rink. Hockey helmets have an outer plastic shell combined with inside foam padding and other functions that can give you optimal protection. Most helmets are adjustable for length and width. It is important that your helmet is the right size for your head; otherwise it will not be as effective in protection.

Shoulder Pads – Shoulder pads are a piece of protective gear that protects your collarbone, chest, shoulders, arms, and back. Many shoulder pads allow you to attach additional lower back protection. Shoulder pads have a broad price range, ranging from $25 for a pair of youth pads to $100 for a pair that will fit an adult.

Elbow Pads – Elbow pads help prevent elbow fractures and bruises on your forearms. Elbow pads are often adjustable and also have a broad price range. Youth elbow pads start at around $20 and $100 for adult pads. You can hold elbow pads in place with Velcro.

Gloves – Hockey gloves are designed to protect your hands from the various hazards of the rink. However, it is important that you wear a pair of gloves that fit correctly to enable your hands to work at their full capacity. Modern day hockey gloves are made out of either synthetic leather or nylon. Synthetic gloves are lightweight and durable. Nylon gloves are also lightweight but are designed for extra breathability. Some pairs of hockey gloves are made out of both synthetic leather and nylon. There are also three different kinds of fits. Anatomical fit gloves provide a snug fit where your hand almost conforms to the glove. Tapered fit gloves, which are the most popular kind, are similar to anatomical fit but offer some wiggle room in your wrist and hand areas. Finally, traditional gloves provide players with a loose fit. Hockey gloves can range in price from $50-$200.

Pants – Hockey pants are designed to protect your lower body from the various hazards on the rink. They are heavily padded and often made from a polyester or nylon outer material with a cotton or foam lining. Like hockey gloves, the size and fit of hockey pants will vary from manufacturer to manufacturer and really just comes down to personal preference. The most important piece of information to know is how to make sure your pants fit right. The bottom of your pants should be able to cover the top of your shin guards.

Shin Pads – Shin pads protect your lower legs from contact with pucks and other players' sticks. Shin pads should fit your lower legs fully from your knee cap to the top of your skates. Shin pads range in padding and flexibility depending on what position you're playing. Players who often block shots should have shin pads with a thick padding while most forwards prefer more lightweight pads that grant flexibility. Again, the price of shin pads range from around $25 for youth pads and $100 for adult pads.

Skates – Hockey skates are one of the main pieces of equipment. To ensure optimal performance, it is important for you to know how to pick the right pair of skates. A skate consists of the boot, which you put your foot in, the plastic holder and the steel runner, which helps mobilize you. The boots are often designed with padding and inserts that can help your foot breathe and stay fully supported. Most boots also come with heel and ankle support. There are many brands of skates out there so the first step in choosing the right fit is to find out your foot shape. The most effective way to figure this out is to measure the length and width of your foot. It is also important to consider the narrowness of your foot. Many brands offer wide and narrow boot options. The best way to find the right fit is to try on different pairs until you find something that fits perfect and is comfortable. Another factor to consider is whether you're buying skates for recreational play or competitive play. Competitive players often aim to purchase high performance skates while recreational players do not need too. High performance skates offer players multiple features, including lightweight materials, durability, and extra padding.

Stick – The stick is the third most important piece of equipment in the world of hockey. Many players prefer to use sticks that have the right "feel," meaning that it enables them to sense and control the puck. The most important things to consider when choosing a stick are material, construction, flexibility and length. Most sticks are made out of wood or composite. Wood sticks often provide the best feel but are not as durable as composite sticks, which provide better shot power and more durability. Sticks are also constructed as one piece or two piece sticks. One piece sticks are lightweight and come with a consistent flex point and shaft response. Two piece sticks enable you to create a customized stick because you can use different shafts and blades.

In terms of flexibility, it all comes down to the shaft and the player. Shafts come with a number from 40 to 110 and stiffer shafts have higher numbers. Stiff shafts are important for heavy players and flexible shafts are better for lighter players. For example, a defense player may benefit from a stiffer shaft than a forward, who does more puck-handling. However, in the end, it all comes down to personal preference. In terms of length, it mostly comes down to age and experience. For example, a senior player would usually do best with a 60" stick while a youth would do best with a 48" stick.

Mouth Guard – Mouth guards are small and cheap and can provide maximum protection for your teeth. Considering that a hockey puck can travel up to 120 miles in the air and impact your teeth at a force of 1,250 pounds, a mouth guard can ensure that your mouth, teeth and head have added protection. Though mouth guards are not mandatory in all leagues, they are required by a majority of leagues. Mouth guards are made out of rubber and can also help prevent concussions, jaw fractures, neck injuries and neurological hemorrhages. Mouth guards come in a variety of sizes and colors and can often mold to your mouth for a custom fit. The average price of a decent mouth guard is around $10.

Jock Strap/Cup – Jock straps or cups are protective equipment for the private parts of a male player. They are often made of a mesh pouch and a hard, plastic outer shell to prevent contact injuries. They also come with mechanisms at the top of the pouch to hold the cup in place. You can easily purchase a jock strap online or at your local sporting goods store. They are fairly inexpensive and depending on what kind you get, they can be as cheap as $15.

Socks – Hockey socks fit over your shin pads and are a good indicator of your team. Hockey socks are often made out of polyester and should be wide enough to fit over your equipment. The best types of socks to look for are those that are made from a lightweight and well-ventilated material to avoid overheating. You will need tape, Velcro or garters to hold up your socks. It is a good idea to have several pairs of socks on hand at a time, as they tend to rip easily. The average price of a pair of hockey socks is about $15.

Jersey – The jersey is a standard part of a hockey uniform. Jerseys vary in color and logos from team to team and help fans differentiate between players. There are three types of jerseys: practice, replica and authentic. Practice jerseys are made out of a thinner material and may or may not have the team markings on them. Replica jerseys are replicas of professional players' jerseys and are built with a more durable material. Authentic jerseys are professionally knit and have fight straps inside of them. Most hockey players own at least two practice jerseys. Your jersey should fit you loosely and should be made out of a lightweight, thin material that will not cause your body to overheat. The price of a basic practice jersey averages at about $15.

Gear Bag – If you have a large amount of hockey equipment to haul around then I would suggest the investment of a gear bag. Hockey gear bags are large, durable bags that have a large middle compartment for your main gear and small side compartments for your smaller accessories. Hockey gear bags generally come with a shoulder strap or wheels for convenient carrying. The average price of a hockey gear bag ranges from about $30 to $100.

Hockey Puck – Pucks are the standard "ball" of the hockey court. A standard puck is made of rubber and comes 1 inch thick and 3 inches wide. The weight of a puck usually ranges between 5 and 6 ounces though it is possible to use a more lightweight puck, which is common amongst youth leagues. It is common practice to freeze a puck before a game to avoid having it bounce on the ice. The home team's logo is often displayed on the top of the puck. Pucks are on the cheap side and are generally priced from $1 to $5. You can also buy a puck bag to keep your pucks together within your gear bag. These bags usually range from $15 to $20 in price.

Goalie Equipment:

Goalies generally wear the same kind of gear as the other players except some pieces are specially designed with more padding. Look for specific items such a goalie leg pads and arm pads, goalie masks and goalie neck protectors. Goalies should also consider having the following gear:

Goalie Mask – Goalie masks are specialized helmets with more stiffness and strength for goalies. They come with a frontal cage that provides the goalie with sharp vision as well as simultaneous facial protection. A goalie mask should provide your face with a snug fit and should ideally be HECC certified. A typical goalie masks ranges in price from $100 to $700 but is an imperative piece of equipment for anyone tending the goal.

Chest Protector – Goalie chest protectors are designed to protect your chest and arms. Most chest protectors are designed with a hard outer shell and a comfortable foam lining. Top of the line chest protectors provide players with top notch protection without ruining mobility. Some chest protectors come with removable pads that you can adjust for a good balance of protection and mobility.

Blocking Gloves – Blocking gloves are special gloves worn by goalies with blocker boards that can help block shots from the opposing team. They also serve to protect your hands while you hold your stick. Blocking gloves can be made out of a variety of materials, including foam, plastic, nylon and synthetic leather. Many blocking bboards are designed with a special angle to protect the net from pucks that roll over it. The angles also help goalies deflect pucks from the goal. Blocking gloves can also come in a flat-style design but that makes it easier for the puck to roll off the gloves and into the net. Blocking boards tend to be thick and durable.

Throat Guards - Throat guards are designed to protect the neck and throat of goalies. There are 2 main types of throat guards: danglers and collars. Danglers, like their name, are hard pieces of plastic that dangle from goalie masks. Collars are made out of foam padding and plastic inserts and are designed to protect against cuts. When sizing a throat guard collar, look for one that covers your throat, neck and collarbone. When sizing a dangler, it is important to select the best cut.

If you're a beginner and you're not sure what to buy or how much to spend, this video by Hockey Tutorial, How to Buy First Ice Hockey Equipment can be a great help!

Chapter 2: The Best Stretches for Hockey Players

Hockey is a very physically intense game which utilizes many of your muscles. Without performing a proper stretching and warm-up routine, you are more likely to injure one of your muscles which could cause you to have a difficult recovery and spend more time off the ice. Injuries can also have a negative effect on your motivation and self-confidence so it is very important to take proactive preventative steps. The best and easiest way to prevent muscle injuries is to stretch before and after you start a workout, practice or game. In this chapter, you will discover the best warm up exercises and stretches for hockey players.

Hockey players are more likely to incur an injury during a game rather than a practice. Research shows that most injuries occur during the last 5 minutes of the game due to fatigue and tiredness. Almost half of injuries occur during the third period. While head and face injuries are most common, almost half of other injuries involve the upper and lower bodies of players. The most common type of injuries is sprains and strains. Forwards and defense players are those who are most likely to incur an injury. Stretching before and after a game is a great way to protect yourself against these statistics. There are many benefits to stretching besides injury prevention. Stretching can also improve your range of motion and posture, boost your strength, muscle durability and relaxation.

The most important muscles needed for playing hockey are your core muscles. This is because of the large amount of energy you transfer from your skates to your trunk. Your core muscles include your abdominal, multifidus, rotatores and hip muscles. You will also use your large latissimus dorsi, deltoid and pectoral muscles. In terms of your lower body, your gastrocnemius, soleus, quadriceps and glutes are all muscles you will utilize in hockey.

Warming Up

Warming up is an important precedent for stretching because it increase blood flow to your organs and muscles, which can help prevent tear and strain injuries that can occur during a stretch. It's also a great way to help you get in the mood for stretching. A warm up usually consists of a set of general exercises that target multiple points of your body from your neck to your ankles. Here is a great general warm-up routine that has worked for me for a variety of sports:

The first way to start your warm up is to perform light aerobics. This includes taking a brisk walk, a slow jog or a quick spin on a stationary bike. You could also march in place, walk up and down a flight of stairs, bounce on a mini trampoline, take a swim or engage in any activity that gets your heart pumping.

Once you've finished performing your light aerobic activity, you can perform a light dynamic stretching routine to continue warming your muscles. These basic movements can help your muscles loosen up even more. Here is a good dynamic warm up routine to follow:

Note: If a warm-up exercise works one side of your body at a time, remember to perform at least one rep for both sides of your body.

Prisoner Squats: Assume a stance that is slightly wider than your shoulders. Rest your hands at the back of your head. Lower your body into a squat and look upward. Squat down as far possible without bending your knees any further. Hold and then push yourself back up. You can jump off the ground when push back up if you choose.

Jump Rope: Rapidly jump up and down while quickly twirling a jump rope underneath your feet. Spring up from the ground using your feet and ankles.

Jumping Jacks: Assume a stance where your feet are together and your arms rest at your side. Simultaneously jump while widening your stance and clapping your hands together over your upper body. Repeat this motion over and over until you feel your heart pumping.

Ankle Bounces: Rapidly jump and up and down, springing off the floor using your feet and ankles.

Walking Lunges: Assume a stance in which you're standing tall with your feet together. Step forward into a lunge and bend both knees at to lower your hips to the ground. Don't let your back knee hit the ground. Put your weight on the foot of the leg you brought forward and use your opposite foot to push off the floor and bring your other leg forward as you step into another lunge.

Side Step Lunge: Bend your knee. Keeping your head, knee and toe aligned, step directly to your side.

Toe Touches: Assume a normal stance. Bend the top half of your body over your legs. Relax and allow your torso to naturally hang in front of you. Allow your arms and hands to hang naturally too, pointing toward your toes for 20 seconds.

Power Skips: Skip rapidly and at full speed as high and fast as you can.

Arm Circles: Assume a normal stance and hold your arms out as if you were getting ready to fly. Start out by slowly swinging your arms to make circles with a one foot diameter as you continue to breathe normally. Swing your arms in a circle pattern for at least ten seconds.

Crunches: Assume a sit up position. Put your hands together behind your head but don't interlace them. Lift your torso until your shoulder blades come up off the floor. Repeat multiple times.

Lateral Leg Swings: Stand and face a wall. Rest your hands on the wall and lift one of your feet slightly off the ground. Swing your leg back and forth about 10 times and then repeat with your left leg.

Pendulum Swings: Lean on a table to support your body. Bend your knees and let your opposite arm hang. Swing it back and forth, side to side and in circular motion at 10 times each and repeat for your other arm.

Shoulder Rolls: You can stand or sit for this warm up. Rest your hands at your sides or on your lap. Breathe in and roll your shoulders backward as you breathe out. Let your shoulders rest and then take another deep inhale and roll them forward.

Run in Place: Perform this warm up for one minute.

Single Leg Hops: Stand on one leg and bend your knee. Stand next to a cone or other kind of marker. Perform a counter-jump and jump sideways over the cone. Land on the leg you pushed off with.

Standing Hip Circles: Balance on one leg. You can hold on to something for support if needed. Bring your opposite knee up to a 90 degree angle and attempt to draw a circle in the air with it. This allows you to open up your hips. Repeat on both sides multiple times.

If you find that any particular muscles are tight, you can run a foam roller over those spots for 10 to 30 seconds and then perform a static stretch, also held for 30 seconds, to loosen them up and return them to their normal length prior to stretching.

Paulwebb.tv has put together a great video on a really good stretching warm up routine that demonstrates most of these exercises, called Full Body Dynamic Warm Up .

Stretches for Hockey

After performing your warm-up routine you can delve right into your stretching routine. Always remember to pay attention to your posture during your stretches. Perform these stretches slowly and only push yourself to the point of discomfort and not pain. Depending on your experience level, I recommend holding a stretch from at least 10 seconds (beginners) to no longer than 30 seconds (advanced).

Trunk and Shoulder Stretch:

This stretch targets your triceps and latissimus dorsi muscles.

-Stand with your feet spread at shoulder width and lift up your chest.

-Raise your right elbow over your head.

-Flex your trunk to the left while simultaneously pulling your elbow to the left with your left hand. This should cause your right hand to move down your back.

-Hold this stretch for up to 30 seconds.

-Repeat with your left elbow.

Standing Quadriceps Stretch:

This stretch works your quadriceps muscles.

-Stand tall and near a wall if you think you'll need something for balance.

-With your back straight, lift your chest, grab your ankle with your adjacent hand, and pull your foot back until your heel reaches your glutes.

-Hold this stretch for up to 30 seconds. Repeat twice and then perform with your other leg.

Hip Flexor Stretch:

This stretch works your hip flexors.

-Kneel on your left knee and put your right foot in front of you.

-Place your hand on your left hip.

-Lean forward, pushing your left hip forward until a stretch occurs.

-Hold this stretch for up to 30 seconds. Repeat twice and then perform on your opposite hip.

Hip Adductor Stretch:

This stretch works your hip adductors.

-Sit down and press the soles of your feet together.

-Make sure your back is straight and your chest is lifted.

-Bend forward and gently press your knees toward the floor.

-Hold this stretch for up to 30 seconds and repeat twice.

Sitting Hamstring Stretch:

This stretch works your hamstrings.

-Sit on the ground and stretch your left leg in front of you. Press your right heel against your leg.

-Lift your chest and keep your back straight.

-Bend forward until a stretch occurs in your thigh.

-Hold this stretch for up to 30 seconds and repeat twice. Perform with your right leg.

Dual Hip Stretch:

This stretch targets both hips as well as your lower back.

-Lie on your back and pull your left knee toward your chest.

-Hold this stretch for up to 30 seconds, repeat twice and perform on your right leg.

Chapter 3: Becoming a Better Hockey Player

There are many tips and strategies that you can experiment with to become a much better hockey player than you currently are. In this chapter, you will discover some of the best and most professional strategies that you can add into your routine to see if you can take yourself to the next level. You will find tips for both offense and defense players as well as tips that can benefit all players.

Learn From Watching Hockey Games

Watch lots and lots of hockey games. Watch live games and watch games through the TV. You can even video tape yourself playing to enable yourself to see how you play from a third person perspective. Experience through playing is important but so is "learning by watching." You may have a few favorite professional players from whom you can learn some great techniques and strategies just by watching them and picking up on their playing patterns and habits. It is also helpful to watch or read interviews from your favorite experienced players, as they often provide exclusive advice.

Turn Off Video Games The Night Before a Game

Colorado College hockey players are not allowed to play video games the night before a competition and for a very good reason - they can actually affect your quality of sleep because the constant screen changes can prevent your brain from going into the correct REM cycle. Though video games are great for developing hand-eye coordination, it is best to avoid them the night before a big game.

Know The Best Shots

The best hockey players know that direct shots are the least likely shots to go into the net. Most successful shots are taken from redirections and rebounds. Knowing that these types of shots are more likely to go in the net can help you develop a better shot strategy and increase your number of shots.

Practice Perfect Positioning

Position is half of the battle to winning a game of hockey because popular offense strategies aim to confuse the defense and break up a position to score an open shot. The point of positioning is to protect certain areas of the ice that the opposing team can easily score from. As long as each player knows his or her position on the ice then it will be harder for the offense to impose any confusion tactics.

Study Your Opponent

Studying your opponent can help you get to know your opponent and enable you to pick up on patterns or cues that will help you predict their plays, strategies, habits, etc. Getting to know your opponents inside-out can help prevent you from experiencing any nasty surprises during an important game.

Make Your Stick Durable

Hockey sticks are an important piece of equipment and they can often run expensive. Since hockey is such an intense sport, it is not uncommon for sticks to break. By making your stick durable, you can become a much stronger player and not have to worry about constantly putting out money for a new stick or a stick repair. Sticks commonly break along the bottom of the blade so one of the easiest and best ways to keep it durable is to tape it up and re-tape it any time you can see the tape coming off. The other part of a hockey stick that breaks commonly is the shaft, usually from impact shots. You can also put tape on the parts of the shaft that commonly come into contact with other sticks. Another way to save the life of the shaft is to take easy slap shots, as those types of shots tend to be high impact.

Always Work on Your Weak Skills

The key to success is to constantly work on improving your weakest skills, whether they are skating, shooting, speed or a combination of anything. Some players may find this difficult during a routine practice so when you have free time, focus on sharpening your weakest areas.

Defense Tips:

Use the Markings on The Rink to Your Advantage

By using the markings on the rink to your advantage, you can better position yourself for a better defense strategy. The four face-off dots on the rink can serve as a rink within the rink because they cover the area around the goals. The best place to be on the ice is within this invisible rink while the offense players take the puck outside. The nets on each end of the ice are always aligned with each other so when you are standing in front of your net, you can look at the net on the far side of the rink to determine where you are positioned. This can help you make sure you're not leaving an open hole for a shot. When defending against opposing forwards, you can use the blue line and circles to determine what kind of action you need to take. Pay attention to the top of the circles to make sure that you're not too close to your net.

Practice a Strong Breakout Pass

A bad breakout pass can lead to a bad start and can even get some players benched. Strong breakout passes feel as great as scoring a goal and can lead to a much better play so always make sure to take an extra second to think about your pass and make it smooth and strong.

Focus on Gap Control

Once the breakout pass occurs it is the job of the defense players to control the gap on the rink. The best way to do this is to catch up to the forwards as quickly as possible after the pass. Prepare yourself to jump into the play if needed and always keep moving to prevent a turnover.

Learn to Analyze Rushes

One of the main roles of a defense player is to analyze the oncoming rush as quickly as possible to make a defense strategy. Depending on whether the rush is one on one or three on one makes a huge difference.

For a one on one situation, the defense player should focus on blocking the puck carrier and not the puck itself. Place all of your emphasis on making sure that the carrier cannot get the puck to the net. Another option is that you can check the carrier to prevent him from making a shot. Treat a "two on two" situation the same as a one on one situation. The only difference is that another defense man should be teaming with you. As for a "two on one" or "three on one" situation, focus on the puck and not the players. Leave the players up to your goalie. Focus on staying between the players so that you can deflect any passes amongst them and try and force them into angles that won't allow them to take effective shots.

Bigger vs. Smaller Goalie

Stereotypical goalies are often bigger in size and many people think that bigger is better because a bigger goalie can take up more room in the net and can provide more reach and range. However, there are many advantages to having a smaller goalie. Smaller goalies are more likely to have more agility and speed. Big goal tenders often create more holes when they drop because their chest and arms move out of the net area. This is less likely to happen with smaller goalies.

Wrist Slap

A good strategy for causing an opposing player to lose the puck is to slap them on the area of their glove that houses their wrist. A medium strength slap can cause the player to lose control of the puck and/or mess up a potential shot, giving your team the opportunity for a steal.

Bump Check

An easy way to "check" another player without too much contact is to simply bump him or her. A bump can cause an opposing player to lose focus which makes it easier for your team to take the puck. A bump also can come off as an "accidental brush" so it works really well as a sneaky move.

Avoid "Cheap Shot" Contact

Any type of contact that will obviously throw a player off focus to the point that he or she can become seriously injured is off limits. Examples of a cheap shot include elbowing or spearing. Not only are these types of physical contact immoral but they can also ruin someone's life and are not worth it.

Use Longer Stick

One good strategy for defense players is to use a stick that is a couple of inches longer than a traditional stick. The longer your stick, the better your reach and it is important to try and keep your stick on the puck at all times.

Develop Strong Communication Skills

Communication as a team is very important but communication among the defense part of the team is especially crucial. If one defense man is doing one thing and the other defense men are not on the same page then the defense strategy as a whole will not work. The best type of communication among defensemen is verbal. Simply let your other team members know what you will be doing so that everyone is on the same page and can work together.

Pass Retrieved Pucks Quickly

Most defensemen retrieve pucks from the corners of the rink but no matter where you retrieve them from, always pass them quickly to the nearest open forward. Doing so can cause the opposing team's forward players to get trapped in the end-zone, which can ultimately open up an opportunity for a rush.

Focus on Backwards Skating and Turning

Defensemen must constantly skate backwards and turn to be able to properly defend their zone so practicing these skills can help you become a solid defense player. Always keep your feet moving when you're skating.

Shoot the Puck off the Ice

The best defensemen can master the skill of shooting the puck 10 to 15 inches off the ice. This skill can also be shared to offense players. This type of shot is the hardest for the goalie to prevent.

Fake the First Shot

Faking your first shot is a great way to throw off the opposing players and goalie because it gives you time to get in a real shot while their reflexes are still tensed up from the initial shot.

Offense Tips:

Take Puck Across Net

If you ever find yourself in a position in which you're headed toward the goal with the puck and you're able to increase your speed, try to take the puck across the net for a score. Many goalies trust their defenders to block shots and will come out of the net to approach the player with the puck. By bringing the puck across the net, you have a better chance of scoring a shot because it will cause the goalie to open up.

Vary Your Rush Speeds

When rushing against your opponents, vary your speed by switching your pace from slow to fast. There are many benefits to a varied rush speed. Overall, it can create confusion amongst the opposing team which can give you an advantage during a tight moment. Varying speeds can cause the defense to lose focus and disband, which can buy you more time to get the puck across the rink. It can also enable your linemen to catch up with you.

Switch Up Your Shot Angle

By switching up the angle from which you take your shot, you can potentially throw off the goalie and make a score. When you have the puck in your possession, bring it out to an angle that is wider than one you would normally take a shot from. This can cause the goalie to line up with where the puck currently is. Then pull it in towards you and quickly take the shot. If the goalie is not fast enough or doesn't see the change in angle coming, your chances are making the shot are much higher.

Eat the Puck

One of the number one rules of hockey is to avoid taking blind shots. If you have possession of the puck, it is better to wait and evaluate your situation rather than just take a random shot and hope that you score. Waiting for the right moment can help you prevent the other team from stealing the puck from a shot that you missed.

Practice Jam Plays

Jam plays are a power strategy in which the offense rushes in front of the net from various angles while keeping the puck in motion and switching their pivot men. The point of this play is to try and free up the goalie though this type of play can be risky because there is not enough defense to save the puck if it goes into a corner or behind the net.

Play With An Invisible Puck

Practicing using no puck can help you and your teammates develop anticipation, which can help improve synergy and teamwork when you're actually playing with a real puck.

Exercise Your Wrists

Strong wrists are more likely to make better and stronger shots. You can exercise your wrists at a gym or you can buy a small wrist exercising tool, such as a squeeze ball, to perform at home.

Shoot Low

Patterns show that players who score the most points often take low shots. This makes sense because goalies traditionally raise their arms to keep the puck from flying into the net. When they make this movement, it opens up a weak spot down below. Though some goalies can quickly change their position to block a low shot, it usually doesn't happen very often.

Master Your Steal

One of the most common ways for a team to gain possession of the puck is to steal it from the opposing team. If an opposing player has the puck, there are several ways to steal it. If he or she has it to the side, you can try to lift his or her stick or try to slide in. If he or she has the puck in the front, a good strategy is to hook his or her elbow to break focus.

Pass the Puck

Passing the puck is the most efficient and best way to move the puck toward your opponent's net. You could move the puck up the ice by yourself but passing it to your open teammates is a much better strategy because it makes it harder for the defense to steal the puck and it utilizes teamwork to score a goal. Without passing the puck, an opposing team member could easily narrow in on you and steal the puck by checking you or calculating a steal strategy by watching your skating pattern. It is much better to work together to move the puck.

Back Check the Player Without The Puck

The best strategy for back-checking is to target the player who is most open and who does not have possession of the puck, especially if the player with the puck is not nearby. This player is of concern because the puck carrier has the option of passing the puck to this open player for a shot. Work with your defenseman to cover both of these players.

Avoid Slap Shots in the Slot

Use either a wrist shot or a snap shot when you're taking a shot from the slot. Slap shots are not the best type of shot to use in this position because they do not provide a good amount of speed or accuracy.

Throwing the Puck Back

When you are throwing the puck back into the zone, shoot it towards the corner or an end board. This makes it more difficult for the opposing goalie and defensemen to take control of the puck.

Chapter 4: The Top 5 Hockey Workouts

Hockey is an intense sport that requires strength from different muscles in different parts of your body. While participating in a general strength training program is important for maintaining your overall strength year-round, focusing on strengthening a variety of your muscles will help you improve different skillsets, including endurance, speed, strength, agility and shot power, when hockey season approaches. In this chapter, you will discover the best workouts for developing each skillset listed above.

#1 Endurance Workout

Endurance and explosiveness are very important in hockey. During a 1 hour game, most players get at least 15-20 minutes of play time in each. Since hockey is a very active and intense sport, building your body to withstand quick and powerful movement is crucial. This workout will prepare your body to train for endurance and explosive movements on the rink.

- **Foam Roller Exercise**

  You will need a foam roller for this exercise. Start out by sitting on the roller perpendicularly. Cross one leg over your opposite knee. When you do this, you should feel an intense pressure in the glutes over your leg. Hold yourself up by placing your hands on the floor and start to roll your glute muscles up and down, deeply. This may even cause your muscles to hurt. Roll as long as you can endure it, ideally 3 to 5 minutes, and then switch your legs and repeat the motion.

- **Skater Strides**

  Secure a resistance band around the tops of your knees and then move your legs apart from each other until you feel resistance. To perform this exercise, step out to the side as far as you can and then bring your other leg towards you. Don't bring it so close that you lose tension in the band but close enough so that your step counts as a stride. One complete step counts as one rep. Perform two sets of 12 reps for each leg.

- **One Armed Dumbbell Snatch**

  Hold a dumbbell in one hand and stand with your feet hip width apart. Allow a natural arch in your lower back. Position yourself as if you were going to perform a deadlift. With an explosive movement, straighten your hips and knees and bring the dumbbell up to your chest. Immediately flip your wrist and extend the dumbbell over you. Return the dumbbell to your starting position by moving in reverse to complete one rep. Perform three sets of 5 reps for each arm.

- **Behind Step Lunge**

  Align your feet with your shoulders and reach your hands out in front of you. Place one hand on top of the other. Perform a lunge as far to the left as possible and lower yourself as deep into the lunge as possible. Reverse the lunge by stepping behind your right leg and position your foot to the right to complete one rep. Perform two sets of 8 reps for each leg.

- **One Legged Squat**

  Stand on a box that brings you about a foot from the ground. Hold two dumbbells and hold them out in front of you. Raise one leg off the box and squat down. Raise yourself back up and place your leg back on the box to complete one rep. Perform three sets of 10 reps for each leg.

- **Swiss Ball Cross Chop (Always perform after one legged squat)**

  This exercise requires the use of a Swiss ball. Hold a dumbbell in each hand and lie on the ball until your knees are bent at 90 degrees. Bend your elbows to 90 degrees and perform a crunch. Raise your arms out as your upper body raises off the ball. Return to your original position by reversing the motion to complete one rep. Perform three sets of 15 reps.

#2 Speed Work Out

This exercise helps you develop quickness and agility. Place a cone on the ground and place 3 more cones 10 meters away. Make sure each of the three cones is spread of 5 meters from each. You will come back to these cones later.

Begin this exercise by performing 15 air squats (insert video here). Once you've completed your air squats, move your focus to the cones.

Stand in front of the cones and stay completely still near the starting cone. With an explosive start, sprint towards the top cone. Touch the cone and then sprint back to the starting cone. Next, sprint to the middle cone, touch it and return to the starting cone. Finally, sprint to the last cone, touch it and return to the starting cone. Rest for two to three minutes and repeat **seven** times. Don't forget to rest for at least 1 to 3 minutes between each set.

To get the most out of this drill, make sure that you keep your body low to the ground. This can help you focus on changing direction, which is another important skill to have in hockey. Try to make your stops and starts short and explosive to really sharpen your agility skills.

To modify this drill and keep it interesting, you can substitute several exercises for the air squats. You could perform sit-ups, jumping jacks, burpees, etc. instead. You can also modify the way you perform the cone drill. You could focus on performing tight turns in between the cones, running backwards, sideways, etc.

Perform this drill about two to three times per week to help you reach peak performance and maintain your quickness and agility skills.

#3 Goalie Drill – Visual Targets

This drill enables goalies to learn how to get used to blocking shots from a variety of different angles. This drill/workout will require two players: 1 goalie and 1 shooter.

Spray paint different lines from different angles in front of the goal. The angles should ideally fan out around the goal and shots should be taken from different distances. The two lines that fan from the goal to the two circles in front of it should have the shortest distance. One player will take shots from various distances, using the spray painted lines as their guide to judge their angles while the goalie works to block each shot.

#4 Skating Work Out

- **Skating Circles**

  This skating workout focuses on developing speed and your ability to turn. Stand in one corner of the rink and start by skating quickly and intensely to the zone's faceoff circle. Skate around the circle while doing crossover turns and then skate toward the other zone's faceoff circle to skate around. Next, skate around the center faceoff dot and the two circles in the far zone.

- **Line Skating**

  This skating workout focuses on developing your footwork. Stand in one corner of the rink and begin by skating quickly and intensely to the blue line at the boards. Stop once you reach the line. Next, skate to the opposite boards and stop. After that, skate to the red line and then skate back to the other side of the rink. Next, skate to the far blue line, then to the corner of the far zone and then return to your starting point. You can also perform this drill in reverse.

- **Sled Dog Skating**

  This skating workout focuses on developing your endurance and skating power. This workout also requires two players. One player skates the length of the rink while holding on to another player, who positions their skates in a snow-plow form. Once the skating player reaches the end of the rink, each player switches roles.

#5 Stickhandling Workout

- **Head Up Drill**

  This drill helps players learn to not look at the puck while they're handling it. This drill requires two players or a player and a coach. Set up a line of cones and have one player skate through the cones with the puck. The other player or coach uses their own stick to keep the other player from looking down at the puck.

- **Soft Hand Drill**

  This drill helps players develop their puck-handling skills. This drill requires two players or a player and a coach and is meant to be done off-ice. Two players should stand a few feet from each other and pass a tennis ball back and forth while handling it backhand and forehand. A tennis ball is more difficult to handle than a puck and that is what makes this drill so effective.

- **One Hand Drill**

  It is not uncommon for a hockey player to have to take his or her hand off the stick during a game. Set up a line of cones along the rink. Weave in and out of the cones while moving the puck with you, using one hand only. Alternate which hand you use.

Developing Your Own Hockey Workout

Depending on your current abilities and skillset, you may need to focus on training for all important areas of hockey or you may just need to focus on one or two areas that need improvement. One of the biggest benefits of creating your own plan is that you can easily work it around your schedule. In this section of this chapter, you will discover how to design your own hockey workout.

Step 1: The first step is to get all of your information organized. I recommend using a calendar that breaks your training season down. The first and most important thing to do is figure out when you'll start and end your training.

Step 2: The second step is to have a clearly defined goal. Consider whether you can work your goal into your calendar. For example, if your goal is to improve your agility you can mark down the date of the time by which you want this to improve and therefore create a visual of just how long you have to prepare. If your goal is to train your leg muscles better then you know to focus more on physical strength routines and not as much actual training on your skates.

Step 3: In this step, you'll want to plan out how and when you will train each month, detail by detail. You'll want to include how much time you plan on spending with on and off the ice, how many games you'll be playing that year, how many times you'll want to play for fun and how many breaks you will take. Calculate how many hours per month you will spend on training so that you can break those hours down day by day.

Step 4: In this step, it is time to break your monthly training hours into weekly hours and then into daily hours. If you want to spend 6 hours in the first week of the month on training, you could plan three one hour training sessions during the week and then a two hour casual ride over the weekend. Make sure to plan in a recovery period every two weeks in which you lower the amount of hours you budget to train.

Step 5: Review your custom work out plan each month. Periodic adjustments may be necessary. For example, if you reach your goal of training your leg muscles than you can make modifications to include more training sessions on your skates and less focus on physical strength exercises. Reviewing is very important because the more consistently you train, the more your body will change.

Chapter 5: Diet and Nutrition

Hockey is a fast-paced sport that demands a great deal of energy from its players. The best way for your body to keep up with this energy is through diet and nutrition. Nutrition is a vital component of athletics. Your diet directly affects your performance and a healthy one is vital for supporting consistent training. Understanding the facts about proper diet and nutrition habits is important for achieving a powerful performance.

Food and water can help enhance your strength, stamina, speed and mental performance. Not only does maintaining a healthy body boost your physical performance, it also keeps fat away. Excess fat on your body can cause your speed, endurance and agility to drastically decrease. As an athlete, it is best to compare your dietary habits to your performance on the field – tackle each one with the same amount of effort. If you focus more on your performance than your nutrition, it will cause an imbalance and you will likely perform poorly. Taking care of your body in the long run can also help you heal quicker if you ever become injured.

By following the right nutritional guidelines, you can provide your body with enough energy for an explosive performance on the rink. The best sources of fuel for athletes come from carbohydrates, proteins and fats. The challenge for players is finding the best ratio of these macronutrients that will allow optimal performance.

Carbohydrates

Carbs are the best source of energy you can provide your body with for cycling. Your body consistently burns carbs through your cycling habits as well as your normal day to day activities so it is very important to provide your body with a diet that is high in carbohydrates. More carbohydrates = more energy. It is important to avoid simple carbohydrates (white bread, candy, etc.) and aim for complex carbohydrates. These carbs can be found in fruits, vegetables and whole grains. Carbs should make up 45-60% of a hockey players' diet. A good guideline is to consume 5 to 7 grams of carbs per every 2lbs of your body weight.

Here are some great sources for carbohydrates:

- Leafy green vegetables
- Kale
- Broccoli
- Cauliflower

- Onions
- Bell Peppers
- Apples
- Bananas
- Berries
- Tomatoes
- Avocados
- Citrus Fruits
- Whole Wheat Bread
- Whole Wheat Pasta
- Oats
- Bran
- Rye
- Beans
- Rice
- Potatoes

Eating a pregame meal prior to playing is a great strategy for fueling your body for optimum performance. Your pregame meal should consist of low-fat foods, as foods high in fat take longer to digest and can make you lag. You can break your pregame meal down into small meals. Start prepping your body for your big game from the moment you eat breakfast. Breakfast is the base meal of your day and many players make the mistake of skipping it.

Start fueling your body with carbohydrates from common breakfast foods such as toast, cereal or eggs. Steel cut oats with fresh berries is another good idea.

Alternatively, you can make a smoothie. For lunch and dinner, it is best to consume grilled meats, vegetables, pasta and a fueling beverage such as a sports drink.

Immediately after performance, or at least within 30 minutes of stopping, you should consume a postgame snack to boost your fluids and carbohydrates. This snack should be a mixture of proteins and carbohydrates. Good examples of a postgame snack include nutritional bars, string cheese, yogurt with fruit, trail mix, rice cakes, pretzels or crackers with peanut butter and a sports drink or water.

After your game or workout, you should eat a postgame meal to refuel yourself. Some good ideas for a postgame meal include steak, rice, salmon, salads, roast beef, potatoes and grilled chicken.

Important Tip: Watch how much caffeine you consume on a daily basis – it can make you hungrier throughout the day. You should also avoid soda. The high content of sugar and carbonation in soda can cause your body to work harder, thus taking away energy you could be utilizing on the field. Additionally, avoid fast food and processed food.

This video by Hockey Tutorial, What to Eat Before Hockey, shows some great examples of what you can eat before, during and after a game.

Stay Hydrated

Staying hydrated is not just important for playing sports. It is important for everyone, every day. Analyzing the playing conditions of the game are is a good way to figure out your hydration needs. If you go too long without drinking water or a sports drink, it is possible to get dehydrated. Left untreated, dehydration can lead to cramping, heat exhaustion, brain swelling, seizures, hypovolemic shock, kidney failure, and in extreme cases it can lead to a coma, stroke or death. The best way to stay hydrated throughout a game or practice is to drink 20 ounces of fluid one to two hours before you start. Drink at least 8 more ounces another 15 minutes before you start. If you're just working out, drink 8 ounces of fluid every 10 minutes.

If you start to feel a sudden onset of dizziness, vomiting, fatigue, weakness, muscle cramps or a headache, you should stop what you're doing immediately and hydrate yourself. If you also find that you are not sweating, you may be dehydrated.

Proteins

Protein is important for building muscle mass. You must track how much protein you consume very carefully because too much of it can actually lead to dehydration. The best guideline is to consume .8 grams of proteins for every kilogram of bodyweight. Fruits and vegetables are great sources of protein and are generally very healthy for your entire body. Most vegetarian dishes contain more than enough protein to achieve this requirement.

The best types of proteins to get are those from dairy sources, such as milk and eggs, because they are complete proteins, meaning that they have enough amino acids to help your body completely recover after a ride. Lean beefs, dark-meat chickens and fish are the best meat sources that contain protein. They also come packed with other important nutrients, such as protein, iron and omega-3 fatty acids, respectively.

Fats

Fats often have a bad rap in the world of nutrition because people mistakenly believe that they are all unhealthy for the body. While some fats, such as saturated or Trans-fats are indeed unhealthy, there are also healthy fats that can actually help you boost your metabolism. Some examples of healthy fats include avocados, olive oil, almonds, other nuts and seeds, all natural peanut butter, flaxseed, tofu, salmon, tuna and an occasional piece of dark chocolate. Healthy fats should make up at 20-30% of your daily diet.

Basic Strength Training Program

A great way to build strength that you can use on the rink is through a basic program of strength training exercises. Performing a basic set of strength training exercises is not the cure-all answer for a complete hockey training program. You will still need to perform drills, work your core muscles and develop certain skills such as stickhandling and quickness, etc. but it is a good strategy for spending your time during the off-season. It is best to focus on regular strength training during the off-season and then move closer to more hockey-specific training as the season moves closer. Pair this training program with proper nutrition for optimal results.

Begin your strength program by engaging in a 10 minute warm-up. You can use the warm-up routine in the stretching chapter or you can create your own mix of warm-up exercises.

1. **Hang Cleans**

   Perform 4 sets of 10 reps with a 2 minute rest period in between.

   This exercise works your upper legs, calves, glutes, forearms, shoulders and trapezius muscles.

   With the bar hanging at your mid-thighs, lean slightly forward, keeping your back straight and grab the bar with a shoulder-width, double overhand grip. Drive the weight forward by extending through your ankles, knees and hips and shrugging your shoulders toward your ears. Once you reach a full extension, shrug aggressively and flex your arms by pushing your elbows up and out. When you achieve peak extension, bring yourself down to receive the bar in a front squat position. Lower yourself into a full squat position. Raise your body back up by driving through your heels until you're back in a standing position.

2. **Squats**

Perform 2 sets of 10 reps and then 2 sets of 8 reps with a 3 minute rest period in between.

This exercise targets your quads, hamstrings, glutes and hips.

Stand with your feet wider than shoulder-width and your toes pointing forward. Straighten your upper body, reach your arms out, and breathe in. Slowly bring your hips back and bend your knee as you lower yourself toward the ground. Keep your chest upright and your back straight as your butt begins to push back. Go as low as you comfortably can. Engage your core and push your body back up through your heels.

3. **Push Press**

Perform 3 sets of 10 reps with a 2 minute rest period in between.

This exercise targets your shoulders, quadriceps and triceps.

Start by flexing your hips and knees while keeping a stationary upper body. Perform an explosive push back up with your knees. Once your hips and knees have reached maximum extension, move your body weight to the balls of your feet and extend the joints in your ankles. Once your heels have reached maximum flexion, push the bar from your shoulders and use your arms to put it over your head by fully extending your arms. Next, lower the bar back to your shoulders, flex your hips and knees again and then straighten them before you perform the upward movement again.

4. **Deadlifts**

Perform 4 sets of 10 reps with a 3 minute rest period in between.

This exercise targets your glutes, hamstrings, lower back, hips, abdomen and upper body.

Stand with your feet wider than shoulder width and point your toes forward. Align your balls of feet with the bar. Bend your knees slightly, grip the bar with your hands slightly wider than your legs and bend forward at your hips. Lift the bar up to your shins. With a flat back and your chest out, look forward, inhale and then exhale as you lift the bar by straightening your legs. Once the bar is past your knees, rest it against your thighs, pause for a moment and then bend forward at your hips again to bring the bar back down.

5. Bent Over Rows

Perform 3 sets of 12 reps with a 2 minute rest period in between.

This exercise targets your middle back, biceps and shoulders.

Begin by holding a barbell with a pronated grip. Bend your knees slightly and bend at your waist while keeping your back straight. Ensure that your head stays up. Exhale and lift the barbell toward you. Squeeze your back muscles at the top, pause and then slowly lower the barbell as you exhale.

Chapter 6: Mental Techniques and Toughness Training

Building mental toughness can help you become a mentally powerful hockey player, who does not allow others to control and influence their emotions and reactions. Instead, you will be able to react positively to negative situations.

Building mental toughness is the first step you should take to strengthen your state of mind on the ice rink. Once you have reached peak mental toughness then you will never believe that anything is impossible. You will have what it takes to reach your maximum potential. It will enable you to focus on your most important goals with a calm mind despite if you are under a great deal of competitive pressure. The more you put yourself in mock scenarios, the more your confidence and self-worth will grow until your mind grows to its ultimate strength! Mental toughness doesn't usually develop naturally so it is up to you and your coach, if you have one, to develop it thoroughly.

Mental toughness requires a combination of first building your confidence and self-worth and then placing yourself in mock situations to gain actual experience. Your mind will not be able to differentiate between a real game and a practice. First and foremost, you can set up different scenarios during a practice in which you would find yourself under pressure. Focus on practicing how you would handle that pressure as opposed to the pressure itself. Your body language can also make a huge difference. Negative body language opens the door for having a poor attitude. Being aware of your body language during a race or competition can help you condition yourself to always carry yourself like you are confident. Keep your eyes on the prize and not the audience as your mind will follow your eyes.

While mental toughness techniques differ from sport to sport, there are three main factors that play into mental toughness for hockey:

1. You must be willing to make sacrifices – for example, out-practicing your competition.

2. You be willing to find a way to win in every situation, no matter what.

3. You must be able to keep your composure and focus in every game.

The rest of the techniques in this chapter will enable you to build mental toughness for hockey and improving your workouts as long as you focus on practicing them and staying consistent with your goals!

Developing a Will to Win

All athletes have a goal of wanting to win but sometimes a loss or setback can discourage you from going after that goal. A "will to win" is the ability to keep going forward despite any obstacles or adversities that stand in your way. It is often a mixture of determination and commitment to winning even if you're on the loosing team. It's more of a matter of "how" you win and not "what" you do to win. The best thing about having a will to win is that it gives you a competitive advantage in the area of mental toughness.

Developing a will to win begins during your practices. Practice as hard as you play. By practicing with a competitive mindset you can begin to turn competitive play into a very useful habit. You must also not wait for the will to win to bestow upon you naturally because it won't – you have to make it happen yourself. It's up to you to take the lead for your team and show them that you're going to take the game no matter what.

Develop Self-Confidence

You have to first develop your self-confidence before you can become a great athlete. Your confidence level often determines your ability to achieve your goals. The more confidence you have, the more likely you will succeed and vice versa. You can have all the physical strength and endurance in the world but you must also have belief. If you believe you can make a three-point shot then you can make it! If you don't, then your chances of making it may be low.

There are many things you can do to build your confidence and belief in yourself. Many of these techniques are simple. For example, you can stand tall, dress well, practice speaking in front of the mirror and practice positive self-affirmations. Surrounding yourself with supportive friends is a great way to boost your confidence. Since hockey is a team sport, that shouldn't be too hard. You and your teammates can support and build each other up to promote each other. An optimistic attitude can also help you achieve and maintain a strong level of confidence. There are a few more things you can do that go hand in hand with hockey:

- Strength training, exercising, and eating healthy are the core foundations for having great self-confidence and being a great athlete.

- Knowing how to use the 80/20 rule to your advantage is an important, core habit that you should learn before trying out any of the next couple of habits. Basically, this rule suggests that you should focus on the most important 20% of what you're working on to increase your peak results by 80%. For example, if you are a well-rounded player whose weakness is blocking shots, focusing on this skill can help you improve your game overall.

- Many people with low self-esteem tend to wallow on negative past experiences. By thinking about times when you felt your greatest, you can use those examples to push forward into the future.

- Learn how to become more aware of when you start thinking negatively and then say "stop," either out loud or internally.

- Meditation is a powerful way to help yourself engage in your thoughts and learn how to control them. Meditation is easy and you can do it anywhere, as long as you dress comfortably and you have a peaceful, quiet place to do it. It can be very refreshing for your mind and it can really help you harness your confidence.

Use Adversity to Boost Self-Confidence

With many sports comes a run in with adversity, usually in the form of an injury, a decrease in your performance, criticism, failure, team conflicts, etc. Adversity is unavoidable in hockey but if you react to it in an open-minded way, you can use it to help you grow your self-confidence. Many players allow adversity to discourage them, which often leads to the path of mentally giving up. They often think that they are such great players that it will never happen to them but it will, eventually. Players who don't allow adversity to get them down are those who are better able to grow and improve.

The best way to use adversity in a positive way is to follow these two important steps:

1. Anticipate Adversity – If you believe that you will never face adversity then you will eventually be in for a nasty surprise. By expecting that you will experience it at some point, you can better mentally prepare yourself for a letdown and plan on how to deal with it before it strikes.

2. Keep Moving Forward – If you victimize yourself due to adversity, you will never be able to move ahead. The best question to ask when adversity strikes is, "What can I do next?" Don't dwell on your set-back – make a plan on how to get past it and continue to grow into a great hockey player.

Focus on Focusing

Many great athletes have one trait in common – the ability to block out all thoughts that are irrelevant to the competition. To be successful, a player must be in the game both physically and mentally. There is often a 3-way battle in your mind that focuses on the past, present and future. The key is to learn how to keep your focus on the present. Focusing on the past will often rehash your past mistakes and failures. Focusing on the future generates too many "what if" questions. To focus on the present means to practice your ability to trust your skills. Focusing on the present enables you to focus on doing your best in that moment.

A great way to practice on sharpening your focus is to think about past competitions (re-watch them if possible) and try to pinpoint the moment at which you appear to lose focus. Then make a list of things that you find to distract you often. Once you have your list, create a mental phrase, such as "keep going," to play in your head every time you run into one of your distractions during a game. By making your focus a number one priority, you can bring out the best in your performance.

Practice Building Your Composure

Sometimes players can let their emotions take control over their attitude and motivation, especially during a competition. It is not uncommon for players to get frustrated or upset with their team members or coaches when someone does something to cause a setback. Losing your cool during a competition can not only cause a conflict amongst your team but it can also make you look immature. There are a couple of things you can do to practice staying calm and composed during a game.

Practicing your composure during a game is another great way to practice building your focus. If you dwell on the fact that a teammate made a mistake then half of your focus is taken away from the present moment, which could affect your own performance and lead to more mistakes. You must also remember that everyone is human and it is okay to make mistakes once in a while. Nobody is 100% perfect and you cannot avoid making a bad judgement or missing a shot.

A great way to redirect your energy is to use it in a positive way. For example, if a team member is unable to block every shot from the goal, it could be a sign that they need more training. Spend your energy on helping that team member improve their skills so that your team as a whole and decrease the chances of making any mistakes.

Relieve Tension and Play Loose

Athletes who are anxious about losing or any other setbacks during a competition often tend to have tense muscles, which can affect their performance. This type of fear also makes it more difficult for you to focus and perform to your peak physical abilities. Many coaches have a routine for helping their players relieve tense muscles, usually by saying a phrase such as "relax," or "stay focused." Players can also help themselves relax and play loose.

First, you should be able to know what it feels like to perform with tight and loose muscles. You can test this by tightening your arm muscles and trying to take shots and then trying again without the tension to see the difference in performance. Once you're able to recognize when you're playing tense, you must then know how to manage that tension. The most common and effective way to help yourself relax is to practice a breathing exercise to help you calm down. The following is a very effective breathing exercise:

Cool Breath Breathing Exercise:

1. Stick the tongue out of the mouth and curl the sides of it up. Your tongue should look like a roll or straw.
2. Lift the chin up pointing to the ceiling.
3. Breathe in using the diagram and draw air through the tongue.
4. Hold the breath for a few seconds, uncurl the tongue and move it back into the mouth.
5. Exhale through the nostrils and move the chin down.

Do this exercise six times and gradually increase to twelve times over time. The more practice you get in, the more ingrained this exercise will imprint on your brain.

Eliminate Pre-Game Anxiety

While it is perfectly normal to experience excitement and butterflies before a big game, some players experience pre-game anxiety, which can lead to a decline in performance. This happens to many players who place strict expectations on their performance. While it is important to hold yourself accountable for your performance, placing too high of standards on yourself can lead you to have expectations of success, which can deal a blow to your self-confidence if not met. It can also cause you to second-guess your abilities before you even begin playing, which can lead to tension and worrying.

Focusing on what you can control rather what you can't is a very productive strategy for staying calm. While it is easy to focus on things that are out of control, such as losing a game or being unable to train due to an injury, the best strategy is to focus on what you can control, which is mainly your attitude. A positive attitude cannot change things but it can definitely help make the situation easier to live through.

Self-belief is also crucial! One of the biggest issues with those who do not succeed is that they do not believe in themselves. They do not think that they are as good as everyone else or that they are not able to do something as well as others. With enough practice and a bit of confidence, you can do anything that anyone else is able to do. Have faith in yourself and you will be amazed at how far you can go. Sometimes a successful person simply has a strong desire and a good work ethic. If you do something enough times you are bound to become an expert at it. As long as you never give up, you are bound to succeed.

Visualization

Visualization is a very powerful technique for staying motivated and achieving success. Think about what your goals and why you want to achieve them. Then, think about what your life will be like once you've done it. For example, if you are working hard as a college hockey player, think about how great your life will be when you're driving an expensive car and living in a mansion once you've signed your first deal with a professional league. Everything you visualize will be different based on your individual goals and your own self. Visualization is something that the top pros in the world do on a consistent basis. Be sure to make visualization a habit that you do every day to dramatically increase your chances of success. You can also visualize a scene as if you were ten to fifteen feet away in the 3rd person. Just allow the scene to flow naturally with you doing everything perfectly to achieve the desired goal.

Visualizing the puck is also a valuable mental technique. Yes, you have spent a lot of time on the ice playing with the puck and shooting it around, but take a minute to just think about the puck. Imagine that you are watching a video of yourself moving with the puck. Visualize yourself in the third person, as if from a video camera about twenty feet away, and see yourself doing your favorite moves and performing flawlessly. The more that you do this, the better you are likely to perform when this situation arises on the game field. Before each game or practice, take ten minutes to do your visualization. This is a powerful strategy that can greatly improve your performance if done consistently. If you are learning a new technique, be sure to visualize yourself doing it over and over.

You can combine visualization with positive self-statements for a powerful effect. Everybody thinks negative thoughts. It is human nature. However, continual positive self-statements can combat those thoughts. Since negative thoughts are so common, you cannot get rid of them completely. Instead, you can use positive words and phrases to make the thoughts more effective. For example, instead of thinking, "Training is tiring me out so bad, I just want to give up," think "No pain, no gain."

247 Hockey shows some great visualization tips specific to hockey in this video, Hockey Visualization Strategy: How To Train Your Mind to Perform on Ice.

Find Self-Awareness

Finding self-awareness can help you pave your road to success as an athlete. True self-awareness enables you to admit your strengths and weaknesses and to recognize your talents and flaws. Athletes often find it hard to come to terms with self-awareness when speaking with their coaches because they don't like to admit their faults to the person who controls their play time. However, being honest with yourself and those who support you can help you improve your practices, develop good playing habits and boost your overall self-confidence. A good way to begin finding self-awareness is to set an accountability goal every two weeks. I have found that a good way to do this is to keep a progress journal. In this journal, write down every positive and negative experience you incur in your athletic career. If it is a positive experience, write about how good you feel about yourself and how it has made you a stronger athlete. If it is a negative experience, write about what you did wrong, how you learned to fix it and how you will make a better decision next time. The best part about keeping all of this in a journal is that it is fun to go back and read it over from time to time to see how far you've come.

Define Your Goals as an Athlete

Without setting a goal, you are very likely to never achieve success, not just in hockey but no matter what you're doing. Your goals serve as the roadmap that keeps you on track. Without goals, you may very well veer off course and be less likely to reach your achievements.

To be motivated for cycling, it is essential to set goals and know what you're going to do to reach them. Without goals, it is very hard to intelligently make a plan to steer your cycling career in the direction desired. The first thing you can do to stay motivated to play and work out is to set goals and review them several times per day. A good and effective idea is to write your ideas down on paper and put them in a place where you can easily review them. When you write something down, you tend to retain it much better. Take a few minutes and write down some goals, if you don't have them already. A good strategy to utilize when making a goal is to make it seem easy. For example: I will easily do my workout four times per week or I will easily increase my number of winning shots by the end of the season.

Be sure to be very specific about your goals and why you want to achieve them. Vague goals leave too much room for guesswork and too many loopholes for laziness. For example, let's say that you write down a goal that says, "I will easily do my workout." Yes, that is a goal and a good one, but it's not specific enough. A workout could mean anything in this case and could easily cause you to say, "Well I walked one mile today so that's my workout," even when in reality, that type of workout will not help you become a better hockey player. Let's take a look at how you could better break down this goal to be much more clear and specific.

"I will easily do my workout."

Okay – so when you have a vague statement like this, start digging deeper. Pretend like your mentor, boss or coach is the person telling you that this is your goal. Visualize your coach saying "You will easily do your workout." Are you just going to nod your head and say, "okay boss!"? Probably not, because you'll likely find yourself scratching your head in perplexity once you go to fulfill that request.

Figure out what parts of the goals you could question to become more specific. For example, if it were me faced with this goal, I would say, "What defines my work out? Am I working out my entire body or just certain parts?" This could lead your coach to reply with, "You will easily do your leg and upper body workout." So now you know specifically which parts of your body you're working out – while your goal is much clearer now, there is more to clarify. If my coach were to say to me, "You will easily do your leg and upper body workout," and I nodded and said okay, I could just do the workout once a week and think I've fulfilled the goal. Let's dig deeper.

Next, I would ask my coach, "How often will I easily do my leg and upper body workout?"

Let's pretend that he or she replies to me with, "You will easily do your leg and upper body workout four times per week." Okay so now we have a specific area of the body and a measurable number but I still see more information that can be broken down. My next question would be, "How many times during those four sessions a week would I work out each body part?" My coach could reply, "Workout your legs twice a week and your upper body twice a week," to which I would reply, "What four days should I pick?" to which my coach could reply, "Monday and Wednesday for legs, Friday and Sundays for upper body."

At this point, the revised goal states, "I will easily do my leg and upper body workout four times a week, working my legs on Mondays and Wednesdays and working my upper body on Fridays and Sundays."

Now we have a very clear and specific goal. I know what body parts I am working out and when. Though I think I would be satisfied with this goal, I could go even deeper and specify at what times and where I will be working on my goal. If I included those details, my goal would read something along the lines of, "I will easily do my leg and upper body workout four times a week in my home gym, working my legs on Monday and Wednesday mornings before breakfast, and my upper body on Fridays and Sundays before breakfast."

Let's just take a look at the goal we began with and the goal we worked into a clear and specific statement one last time just to make a comparison:

1. I will easily do my workout.

2. I will easily do my leg and upper body workout four times a week in my home gym, working my legs on Monday and Wednesdays before breakfast, and my upper body on Fridays and Sundays before breakfast."

Which goal do you think you would be more successful with? That was just one example. Make your vision compelling and something that really excites you. Too many people make small goals that lack passion, don't be afraid to dream big and shoot for something truly incredible. I could make one more modification to the aforementioned goal to make it truly incredible...

"I will easily do my leg and upper body workout four times a week in my home gym, working my legs on Monday and Wednesdays before breakfast, and my upper body on Fridays and Sundays before breakfast, until I can barrel through a workout without feeling exhaustion."

Now that's what I call a truly complete goal! Once you know what your goals are, the next thing to do is to develop an action plan. It's easy to set a goal. I just made up that workout goal in five minutes and it was easy as pie. Anybody can make up a goal, just as I just did. The true challenge and differential factor is whether or not anyone can actually achieve those goals. Creating an action plans helps you remain self-accountable and actionable in moving toward goal achievement. Now, you will discover what it takes to create your very own action plan.

The first step is to plan a deadline for your goal. Using the workout goal as an example, I would need to find a time and place to get started. Let's pretend that I don't have a home gym, so what would I do then? I would need to find a place to do my workout. This may entail me researching gym memberships in my area or investing in actually creating a home gym. I also stated that I wanted to do the workout before breakfast, so I would have to make sure I actually have an available time slot before breakfast. Let's say that I have to go to work at 9 am every day and I eat breakfast at 8 am so instead of getting up at 7 am I may have to set my alarm for 6 am. The key is to first start working out all of the details that will get you started off on your path to achievement. If I don't take those steps, then I probably won't be setting up a workout routine.

The second and most important step, in my opinion, is to set a completion date for your goals. Without an end date, you're more than likely going to fail to achieve your goal. For example, let's say a manager at a grocery store asks their employees to rearrange the cracker section. If he doesn't say that it needs to be done by Friday at 5pm then it is likely the employees will not look at the task as a priority and it will probably never get done.

Using the workout goal as an example, I stated that I would do it "until I can barrel through a workout with feeling exhaustion." In my case, my end date is a moment of achievement. So until I feel that breakthrough moment where I say, "Hey, I pedaled for two hours and I feel awesome," I will not have reached my goal. Good ways to measure goal completion are to set a time and a date, like in the grocery store example, or to set a feeling, like in my workout example. For a truly challenging goal, you could set yourself to feel a certain way by a certain time and date, which may mean that you have to really focus hard on your goal within a certain amount of time.

You may find it easier to break your goals down into smaller goals for an easier achievement time. A good example of this is to set weekly or monthly goals before you set an ending time and date. For example, I want my goal to be able to barrel through a workout without feeling exhaustion so I might start out by being able to practice for 30 minutes without those feelings and then work my way up to an hour and so on. Those smaller accomplishments can help me feel motivated to keep going until I reach my final outcome. It is not possible to achieve a huge goal overnight so breaking it down into smaller tasks/milestones is actually a really great strategy to try. I'm a particularly self-motivated person so I find that when I make small accomplishments, it pushes me to keep going as far as I can push myself.

Finally, I recommend reviewing your action plan at least once a week. The best strategy is to write it down in a word document and make it a living and breathing article. State your goal, break it down as deep as you can, write down when you hit milestones, restate your goal, track your progress, etc. Your action plan should develop along with yourself. That way you can keep track of just how far you're coming as well as look back to where you started and use it for motivation to keep pushing yourself.

So now you know how to set a goal, narrow it down to specifics, and then turn it into a plan of action. There is just one more component to this formula and that is figuring out why your goals matter. If you are not sure why you set the goals that you set for yourself, you may not feel as motivated to work toward them and you'll have set goals and created a plan for nothing. By asking yourself *why* you want to reach your goal, you can be reminded of its true purpose.

The power of asking the question "why" can make a big difference in helping you achieve success. Many people do not need a tangible award to find satisfaction. Often times, they become inspired to do something just for the enjoyment it brings them or others. Imagine if you asked yourself, "*Why* do I work out hard?" your answer may be, "Because I want to fill up my trophy room with cycling trophies." Why do you work two jobs? "Because I want to be able to afford the best cycling equipment." Whenever you ask "why" you want to do something, it should be followed with an answer that starts with, "Because..."

When you were a young child, you probably asked your parents, "why?" many times. It was because you wanted to better understand how things worked. However, learning is never-ending, and even as an adult, you can still use the question "why?" to gain a deeper understanding of how things work. By gaining a deeper understanding of how things work, your chances of feeling more inspired to move towards your goals will likely be much higher.

So, anytime I feel tempted to take a day off of my workout, I would make myself think about *why* my goals matter. More than likely, that will help me stay motivated, it always does. I can't stress enough how important it is to make your action plan a living and breathing document. Not only does writing your goals down more likely to cause you to achieve them but it can help you figure out why they matter and it can enable you to brainstorm and organize your thoughts on your goals. You may end up coming up with several great reasons for each goal, which can push you even further to pursue your dreams.

Developing Performance-Based Goals

Performance-based goals are goals that are measurable. Quotas and budgets are good examples of performance-based goals. Many people find performance-based goals to be extremely motivating because it gives them measurable results to work towards. It is easy to set performance-based goals for hockey and any sports because there are many factors that you can measure. For example, you can measure your strength and your weight. If you are having problem setting and achieving goals, see if you can turn your goal into something that is performance-based for more motivation.

No More Excuses

Excuses are a big reason that many athletes fall into the groove of becoming unmotivated and unsuccessful. When you continually make excuses for why you are not progressing toward your goals, you will likely never achieve success. A good way to catch an excuse is when you hear yourself saying, "but." Whenever you hear or feel that word coming off your tongue, stop yourself and don't let it come out.

For example, if you hear yourself saying, "I really want to eat this fast food but I also really want to keep my energy levels consistent..." immediately recognize that you're making an excuse for not sticking to your goal. Another good idea is to use reverse psychology on your excuses. For example, you could say, "I really want to eat that fast food *but* if I do that, I won't reach my goal of becoming a powerhouse."

Do Not Fear Competition or Failure

Fear is an emotion that everybody experiences, not just athletes. However, for athletes, fear can often hold them back from their triumphs. Fearing failure can hold you back but in a way, it can also drive you to achieve your goals. The key is that you should not fear failure itself. If the fear of failure prevents you from even trying, then it is holding you back. If the fear of failure causes you to think of what kind of person you will be in the future, it can drive you. For example, let's say that you'd like to be the provider for your family and be able to afford nice things, including a house in a nice neighborhood, and your goal is to do this by becoming a well-paid, professional athlete. In this case, failure to you is not being able to provide for your family by not becoming a professional athlete. You fear this, therefore, you are driven to achieve your goal. If you fear failure itself, in this case, you will likely not even try to become a professional athlete out of the sake of embarrassment, and you will likely not be able to be an affluent provider.

Another good idea is to learn to handle rejection. Having to deal with rejection is inevitable because at one point or another in your life, you will probably be turned down- whether you're rejected from a sports team, a college, a position, or anything else. Many people tend to let rejection discourage them, but if you can see it in a positive light, you can be much better off for the next opportunity. If you are rejected for something, view it as an opportunity to see what you can improve upon. Also, don't get all emotional if someone gives you criticism. They are usually just trying to help and if you can learn to take criticism without blowing your lid, then you will be much better off in your journey through life.

Create a Pre-Game Routine

Many successful athletes develop a performance ritual to help them prepare for a big performance. A ritual is a series of steps that you take before a "big moment" to help you get into the right mental and emotional state of mind. There are two ways to utilize a performance ritual – beforehand and during the moment. In basketball, players get multiple breaks in between periods so you can use that time to focus on your ritual. What you include in your ritual and how you perform it is entirely up to your own imagination but here are a few popular things that most athletes include in their own:

Before the Game:

- Eat a meal at a pre-planned time
- Double-check your equipment
- Visualize your success
- Scope out the venue you'll be playing in
- Wear clothes that give you a high self-esteem
- Record and re-watch your best games
- Spend some quiet time with yourself

In Between the Game:

- Do stretches to distract yourself from negative emotions
- Visualize your success
- Speak with your coach

- Use positive self-talk

- Speak with players who support you

Once you have figured out your personal performance ritual, create a game plan in which you put it all together and try it out. Have a few alternatives practices in the back of your head in case one doesn't work out and always try to keep a consistent schedule so that you don't incur last minute changes or rushing, which may upset your ritual.

Conclusion

I hope this book was able to help you to discover how to become the best hockey player possible.

Hockey is a great sport for all ages and can be enjoyed by anyone for recreational or competitive purposes. Not only is it a very fun sport but it's also very intense, making for a great work out. Anyone can learn how to play hockey and anyone who wants to rise to the top can with all of the information provided to you in this book!

The next step is to identify an area in which you need improvement to start your development. Do you need to work on building a warm-up routine? Perhaps you need to revisit your eating habits and nutritional knowledge. Maybe you need to get better at strength training or practicing your speed, agility, shooting and skating drills.

Figure out where you are and ask yourself where you need to be. Then you can refer to whatever chapter you believe can benefit you the most. Keep going through each chapter, trying each tip or skill, until you believe that you are the most unstoppable hockey player in the world!

Finally, if you discovered at least one thing that has helped you or that you think would be beneficial to someone else, be sure to take a few seconds to easily post a quick positive review. As an author, your positive feedback is desperately needed. Your highly valuable five star reviews are like a river of golden joy flowing through a sunny forest of mighty trees and beautiful flowers! *To do your good deed in making the world a better place by helping others with your valuable insight, just leave a nice review.*

My Other Books and Audio Books
www.AcesEbooks.com

Popular Books

BASEBALL
BASEBALL STRATEGIES
THE TOP 100 BEST WAYS
TO IMPROVE YOUR
BASEBALL GAME
ACE McCLOUD

GOLF
GOLF STRATEGIES
The Perfect Swing
Golf Game Preparation
Ace McCloud

SOCCER
SOCCER STRATEGIES
The Top 100 Best Ways To Improve Your Soccer Game
Ace McCloud

ENERGY
Discover How To Increase
Your Energy Levels
Using The Best All Natural
Foods, Supplements
And Strategies For A Life
Full Of Abundant Energy
Ace McCloud

FOOTBALL
FOOTBALL MADE EASY
BEGINNER AND EXPERT STRATEGIES
FOR BECOMING A BETTER
FOOTBALL PLAYER
Ace McCloud

MOTIVATION
MASTER THE POWER OF MOTIVATION
TO PROPEL YOURSELF TO SUCCESS
Ace McCloud

LOSE WEIGHT
THE TOP 100 BEST WAYS
TO LOSE WEIGHT QUICKLY AND HEALTHILY
Ace McCloud

SELF DISCIPLINE
Unleash The Power Of Self Discipline, Influence And Willpower In Your Life To Achieve Anything
Ace McCloud

Ace McCloud
HABIT
The Top 100 Best Habits
How To Make A Positive Habit Permanent
And How To Break Bad Habits

ATTITUDE
Discover The True Power Of
A Positive Attitude
Ace McCloud

ULTIMATE HEALTH SECRETS
HEALTH
Strategies For Dieting, Eating Healthy, Exercising, Losing Weight, The Mediterranean Diet, Strength Training, And All About Vitamins, Minerals, And Supplements
Ace McCloud

HOCKEY
HOCKEY MADE EASY
BEGINNER AND EXPERT STRATEGIES FOR
BECOMING A BETTER HOCKEY PLAYER
Ace McCloud

Be sure to check out my audio books as well!

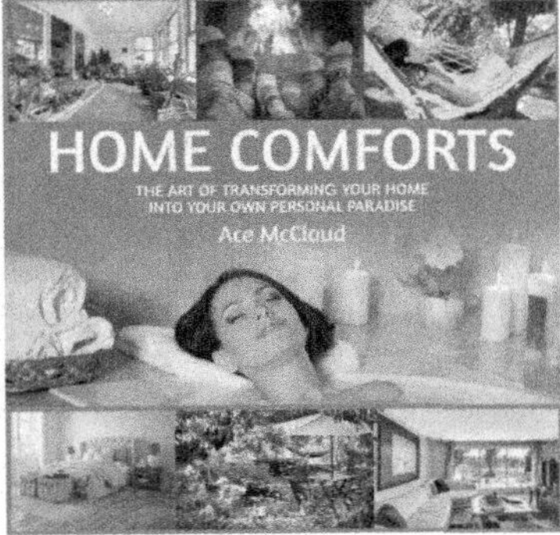

Check out my website at: **www.AcesEbooks.com** for a complete list of all of my books and high quality audio books. I enjoy bringing you the best knowledge in the world and wish you the best in using this information to make your journey through life better and more enjoyable! **Best of luck to you!**

CPSIA information can be obtained
at www.ICGtesting.com
Printed in the USA
BVOW04s0227180917
495152BV00003B/92/P